# NAPKIN FOLDS &
# TABLE SETTINGS

## OTHER NO NONSENSE COOKING GUIDES

*Appetizers, Hors d'Oeuvres & Salads*
*Best Barbecues Ever*
*Breakfasts & Brunches*
*Cookies for Holidays & Every Day*
*Entertaining at Home*
*Fabulous Desserts: Mainly Microwave*
*Microwave Diet Cooking*
*Microwave Main Courses, Quick & Easy*
*Microwave Vegetable Dishes & Snacks*
*Muffins & Quick Breads*
*Pasta Made Easy*

## OTHER NO NONSENSE GUIDES

*Financial Guides*
*Real Estate Guides*
*Legal Guides*
*Health Guides*
*Success Guides*
*Parenting Guides*
*Student Guides*
*Wine Guides*

# NO NONSENSE COOKING GUIDE ®

# NAPKIN FOLDS &
# TABLE SETTINGS

## IRENA CHALMERS

WITH
ELIZABETH LAWRENCE AND MOLLY SIPLE

ILLUSTRATED BY DANA BURNS

**LONGMEADOW PRESS**

NAPKIN FOLDS & TABLE SETTINGS

Copyright © 1989 by Irena Chalmers

Published by Longmeadow Press, 201 High Ridge Road, Stamford, Connecticut 06904. No part of this book may be reproduced or used in any form or by any means, electronic or mechanical, including photocopying, recording, or by an information storage and retrieval system, without permission in writing from the publisher.

No Nonsense Cooking Guide is a registered trademark of
Longmeadow Press

ISBN 0-681-40702-6

Printed in the United States of America

0 9 8 7 6 5 4 3 2 1

### STAFF FOR NO NONSENSE COOKING GUIDES

EDITORIAL DIRECTION: **Jean Atcheson**
MANAGING EDITOR: **Mary Goodbody**
COVER DESIGN: **Karen Skelton**
ART DIRECTION & DESIGN: **Helene Berinsky**
ASSISTANT EDITOR: **Maurice Goodbody**
COVER PHOTOGRAPH: **Matthew Klein**
TYPESETTING: **ComCom, Allentown, Pennsylvania**

# CONTENTS

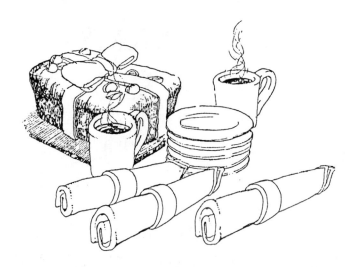

# NAPKIN FOLDS & TABLE SETTINGS

Entertaining is a basic social art, one that encompasses everything from serving supper to the family gathered around the kitchen table to giving the most elegant of dinner parties. "Setting" the table means much more than just putting out food on it for people to enjoy; it is literally a way of creating an atmosphere, just as lighting and staging does in the theater. The occasion may be something as simple as a pleasant ritual gathering for a family meal or the casual welcoming of friends to your home for an impromptu supper. It does not have to be elaborate or obtrusive to be effective, although for many occasions a grand display is just the ticket.

Any table benefits from having had care taken to make it interesting. This is obvious when we think of dinner parties, when putting one's best foot forward is the rule. Not so obvious is the attention to detail, even the simplest, worth paying to make even everyday functions genuinely enjoyable.

There is no law that says you have to buy everything new in order to entertain. You can build your collection of equipment, tableware as well as decorations, gradually. With a little thought and imagination you can come up with all kinds of decorations using items you already have, or can find easily and inexpensively. Some of the most effective table decorations are to be found around your house and in the yard, not to mention the local flea market and tag sales, as well as the department stores and specialty shops.

We all make natural associations in our minds of certain decorating elements for the year's special occasions. Christmas is a time of green boughs and red berries and flowers. Thanksgiving means autumn colors, turkeys and pumpkins. Valentine's Day abounds with red and pink hearts. Easter brings forth yellow ducklings, white rabbits and lambs, and eggs dyed in the colors of the rainbow. The Fourth of July conjures up images of sparklers and fireworks, red, white and blue bunting, gigantic watermelons and picnic food.

Atmospheres, in fact, are created in many different ways. If you want to set an easy, relaxed mood, to arouse a sense of excitement and splendor, or simply to offer a rollicking good time at a kids' party, all the ingredients are blended in the setting you supply: the fragrance of the house as the front door swings open, the music you are playing, the way the light beckons guests into the dining room (or the kitchen), the colors, the decorated table, the artfully folded napkins. . . .

This is a cooking guide that is not about cooking at all. It is about all the other elements that are concerned with offering food in your home to your family and friends—because the way you present your food is what makes it yours, and no one else's. You can make a dish in exactly the way you learned from your mother or duplicate a recipe from the local paper, you can re-create a centerpiece you admired in a magazine or incorporate a tip that worked for a friend—but the way you use *your* china and glassware and linens, *your* special decorations and combinations of colors and shapes

*Use bandannas in a basket to match the old-fashioned feeling of a picnic on the grass with chicken in the hamper.*

to welcome guests to your table for each individual occasion is uniquely yours, and will be different every time.

In addition to illustrating in detail some of the simple folds that make napkins such a stunning addition to your table, this book also contains helpful information and advice about how to plan your decorations, what china, glassware, flatware and linens you will need for entertaining, and how to care for them. If these notions and tips that have worked for us strike off some fresh ideas for you, so much the better.

Setting a table is really very simple, and need only be expensive when you want to make it so. Provided you have all the utensils required for people to eat in reasonable comfort, and have understood the basic logic that governs place settings, you can be off and running in whatever direction takes your fancy.

Don't forget the napkins, though—their elegant folds or jaunty colors are the secret element that convinces every guest that you really have the master touch. (And you don't have to reveal that you learned it from this book.)

# CHAPTER 1

# THINKING ABOUT TABLE DESIGN

Entering someone's home instantly arouses a host of subconscious impressions: smell, color, warmth (or the reverse), light, and the sound of talk and laughter that indicate people are enjoying themselves. You cannot take complete responsibility for the quality of the company and of the conversation, but by thoughtful, careful planning you can do a great deal to bring about the good times.

There is no one way to set an attractive table because the way you do it expresses *you* at that moment, for that particular purpose. You may or may not have made the food you serve, but your personality will always grace the table you set. The cunning touch of a green leaf or the last button chrysanthemum from the window box, a figurine from your treasured collection of owls, say, or a child's handmade placecard beside each setting will do more than bone china or the shiniest sterling to show you forth to your guests. The table should look as if *you* are present even though the room might be temporarily empty.

It is a good idea to begin by looking at your own attitudes—how you feel about feeding people. Are you a warm-hearted, nurturing type of person or a dramatic, more hard-edged entertainer? Be true to yourself. If you like a soft, romantic style, don't feel you have to create a table that is chic, cool and modern-looking. If you are an urban sophisticate, sleek modern designs and dramatic geometrics will be natural choices. If you like informal and provincial looks, choose peasant designs and small floral patterns in tableware. You can also include elements of each style in what you buy or acquire which enables you to play one off against the other or create a different feeling now and again.

Starting with plain things has the advantage of enabling you to go either way. A plain white service of china can be dressed up with formal accessories such as cut crystal, fine linens and silver serving pieces, or down with informal ones such as blown glass and homespun fabrics. You can give heavier, informal stoneware a "company" look with fine-quality glass and linen and a delicate, sophisticated centerpiece of flowers. Sensational accessories—high-style sculptured bowls and plates, for example—can lend almost anything a touch of class.

Food presented in a graphic way can help, too. The more graphic-looking the food—it might be striped, perhaps, or cut into geometric shapes—the bolder your setting will look. Don't forget to add the colors of the

Make a vegetable bouquet by taking bare curly willow branches and skewering them with miniature cherry tomatoes, pattypan squash, red and green peppers—arranged like flowers.

various foods to your artist's palette as well. Choose the dishes and glasses you select for serving in colors that show off the foods as effectively—and invitingly—as possible.

## PLANNING THE EVENT

The purpose of decorating tables is to enhance the mood you want to create, and the secret of success in this, as in so much else, is to have spent time thinking about what you are doing and understood its needs. What kind of party are you planning? Should it be a cocktail party, a picnic, a dinner, a supper, or a brunch? Each has its requirements.

The kind of event it is tells you a number of things. A small dinner party, for instance, is focused around a single table. Conversation is close, so the table should be set up to encourage people to talk freely. If you are giving the dinner for friends, it may be comfortable and cosy. If it is a business party, its style may be more general and less personal.

A cocktail party, of course, is likely to be general, with people standing and moving around a good deal. Your decorations will need to be more diverse—a centerpiece on the buffet table, with other decorations probably placed elsewhere, too.

Don't forget miniature vegetables: tiny carrots and squash look marvelous in small, neat arrangements.

## THE TIME OF DAY

The time of day of a party makes a contribution to your planning. A luncheon or brunch, for example, has no place for candlelight and thereby candlesticks on the table. It is also difficult to spotlight a flower arrangement or other decorative element when natural light prevails. You might, in fact, want to move your table to take the best advantage of the natural light in the room. Your decorations would be lighter, too, using pale colors and light textures in both china and linen.

An evening party, on the other hand, lends itself easily to drama, with contrasts of light and dark colors and plenty of options in lighting variations.

A morning event such as breakfast or an early brunch calls for simplicity in all things. Elaborate settings can be confusing to people who are still a bit groggy from sleep. Most people think of morning, and therefore breakfast, as bright and sunny. It is better to achieve this effect with cheerful colors and bright flowers, however, than by moving your table into direct sunlight; you don't want your guests to have to peer at each other beneath shading hands and those shafting rays can melt butter very quickly.

## WHO WILL BE THERE?

When you know your guests well, you can be relaxed. Maybe you have an impish sense of humor that can be shown in the clever way you decorate your table. With people you don't know you may want to be a little more reserved, showing your personality, by all means, but not so intimately as with close friends. A party that will include children needs, of course, to be geared toward family concerns. Using your best china and linens may make the other parents nervous, too.

Tag sale treasures such as cut glass dressing table jars, covered bowls, mirrored placemats and all kinds of pitchers make great centerpieces, too.

# USING SPACE

Use the space you have available to the best advantage. If your dining room is small, you will want to focus on small gatherings. If the table itself is small, your decorations and place settings should be in scale so that diners have room to eat comfortably without having to compete with the elements on the table.

If both the room and the table are generously proportioned, you can take a more dramatic approach, using big bowls, multiple candlesticks and several arrangements of flowers or objects you have collected.

In setting up a buffet, consider the traffic patterns carefully. Do you have room to set the table in the center of the room and have people approach it from two sides? It may make more sense to move it back against the wall and have guests walk around the three sides from left to right, say, serving themselves as they go. Will there be space to set up an extra table, perhaps, to hold plates and silverware? If setting a centerpiece on the buffet table could make it look crowded, you might plan to decorate other surfaces, such as window sills, the mantelpiece, or occasional tables.

When space is short, condiments arranged on a beautiful tray can double as a centerpiece.

# CONSIDER THE SEASONS

Summer parties call for light and airy decorations, winter ones are usually occasions for coziness and warmth. A room lit with a dozen candles in winter looks cordial; on a hot summer night it could seem stifling.

In summer, bring the outside in by opening doors and windows, allowing the scents of the garden to infuse the room. In winter, nothing says Welcome more immediately than a fire crackling in the hearth.

Use light colors for spring and summer, of course, darker ones for fall and winter—while white is right at any time of year. Bright colors can go either way—to

---

##### WHAT GOES WITH WHAT?

Ethnic and hearty foods such as Mexican food, Indian dishes, or stews and casseroles look great when served in and on brightly colored pottery or terracotta stoneware.

Though barbecued ribs certainly do not belong on your French porcelain, lighter food definitely does. Don't save your best china only for the most elaborate of meals. That delicate porcelain might look delightful serving a simple breakfast or a grilled chicken and salad lunch.

---

brighten up fall and winter parties or to capture the vividness of summer days.

## DECORATING THE TABLE

The centerpiece is often the primary decorating element of a table. It can be a discreet round bowl of flowers from the florist, which of course is the easiest, if not the most imaginative route to take. It can also be a swath of flower petals or a scatter of peanuts in their shells strewn down the center of the table. If you delight in arranging flowers, so much the better. But it is the concept that matters, and with a good concept your chief need is an eye that can tell you when something looks right and when it could benefit from a little rearrangement.

### FLOWERS AND FOLIAGE

If you have a garden, rejoice and make use of it. Cut both flowers and foliage and make your own bouquets and sprays. You may want to work with a mass of color or select single blossoms. You can set a big bouquet in the center of the table or place an individual flower at each setting.

If you can, shop at wholesale flower markets when you are giving a party; many of them sell retail and offer good prices on large bunches of flowers.

Statues and
figurines can
figure on your
table, artfully
arranged, with
one or two
elevated on a
small stand, or
with a large piece
featured and
smaller ones
grouped around.

When blooms are sparse, green leaves and grasses can look lovely, too. In the fall, take colored leaves and dried vines and use them both as bouquets and as accents.

Small potted plants and herbs or flowering houseplants can be lined up on a table very effectively; a large one can be the sole centerpiece.

Remember that if guests are seated around the table, they should be able to see across it easily. A high centerpiece must be light and airy: fresh birch twigs bearing spring's first catkins, for example, or slim, delicate freesias. Or you can use low, floating arrangements of flowers on leaves in a wide glass bowl; pair a rose with a violet leaf, for instance, for a change of pace.

Try scattering extra flowers from an arrangement directly on the table. Set small vases of flowers in a row down a long table, or place them between the settings or circled in the table's center.

### SOME USEFUL ACCESSORIES

· Use American crafts such as hand-thrown pottery bowls, glass dishes and woven baskets to display and carry foods.
· Footed trays and plates are most useful, especially for displaying buffet foods. Elevate condiment bowls on a lacquer footed tray for a Japanese look.
· Tin and wood boxes can hold flowers, breadsticks or crackers.
· Stones and colored or clear marbles make effective frogs for a flower arrangement when placed in the bottom of a glass vase or container. If you like, you could be witty and use cranberries or cherry tomatoes instead of the marbles.
· Woven wicker, fabric or metal baskets make ideal holders for eggs, fruits and vegetables, and breads, as well as flowers. If you like, you can mingle the contents, sticking violets between the brown eggs, for example, framing fresh rolls with brilliant asters, or having yellow daisies spring from a basket of blueberries.

## FRUITS AND VEGETABLES

Heap fruits and vegetables in a bowl or basket for a sumptuous look. You can use lemons, limes, apples, peaches, cherries, pears, strawberries—almost anything that is fresh and has the color you are seeking. You can use vegetables such as artichokes, peppers of all colors, leeks, carrots with their green tops, onions. Once you *really* start looking, there is nothing of good quality that is not beautiful in its own way.

## SOME IDEAS TO ADOPT OR ADAPT

Tie breadsticks or spaghetti around the middle to look like a sheaf of corn. Stalks of wheat can give the same effect.

Baskets of interestingly shaped rolls, breads and crackers can look dramatic, and be practical at the same time.

Use big tropical leaves as placemats for other decorations for food at a buffet, or even as the place-setting mat. Arrange skewers of fruit or other foods on Ti leaves from the florist—long, narrow and deep green—or on palm fronds or fresh ferns.

Scatter nuts and berries such as cranberries directly on a table. The nuts can be eaten; often the berries can, too, and people will start nibbling almost without noticing.

Hollow out melons in a decorative pattern to serve as bowls. You can fill them with bright flowers, such as zinnias, to make centerpieces to be admired, or with fruit salad, to be eaten.

Vegetables grouped in a basket look generous—like a gorgeous market basket filled with good things. Kale, purple cabbage, and other greens make leafy centerpieces. Brussels sprouts still on the stalk can be found in season at many specialty shops, and if you peel back the sprouts to look like flowers, two or three make a very dramatic statement.

# CHAPTER 2

# ESSENTIAL EQUIPMENT

We all know people who can create a dramatic and gorgeous-looking table, from apparently nothing at all. A single flower, a ribbon, just the right dessert plates—and you feel that you are in the presence of genius. Most mere mortals, however, need equipment to set a pretty table. Even the person who favors the minimalist look of a gleaming surface bare of anything but absolutely essential eating utensils needs some "things"—china, silverware, serving pieces, glassware and linens.

At party-time, when you find yourself faced with missing cutlery and plates, mysterious stains on your best tablecloth, and the apparently inevitable choice between changing the menu or serving soup with straws, the knowledge of having made wise choices in terms of these basic equipment needs can save a lot of frustration.

# China

The most important element to consider when selecting china is your own personal taste. Whatever you buy, it must be something that you really like and will use, and that suits your needs, present or future. Choosing a pattern just because the price is right or you think you *ought* to have it is not the way to approach the decision. If you are buying casual china, for instance, remember that you will be using it every day, so you will want something that you won't tire of easily. If you are buying more formal china, consider that you will be using it for years to come, and that the appeal of the trendiest of today's patterns may wear thin before long.

## AVAILABILITY

Whether you are choosing a basic set of china or a more formal pattern, always consider its availability. If you are not ready to invest in something expensive and long-lasting—the kind of set you replace pieces in or continue adding to—there are plenty of good, simple designs available at a modest price. If you want to be able to keep your set complete, however, you might want to choose an open-stock pattern, which will be available for years to come. The advantage of choosing such a pattern is that you can not only replace the pieces that inevitably get broken but can add to the service gradually—a vegetable dish now, some soup plates later on. . . .

## CREATING YOUR OWN SET

With money and time available, anybody can collect an entire set of dishes in one pattern. Creating a set from varied components that show off the different courses of a meal to their best advantage yet still share a common theme or thread takes more thought, as well as time and effort.

There is no law that says the china you use for the soup course *must* appear in each successive course through dessert and coffee. People lucky enough to have a variety of china choose patterns that coordinate for serving different courses. These need not necessarily be of the same pattern family. You might choose to use green glass or majolica leaf plates for salad, for example, then serve the entree on a white plate with a touch of green, and use a different plate—perhaps an antique that picks up one of the colors, shapes or decorations from the other dishes—for the dessert. The serving pieces can be coordinated as well. This adds interest to the table and invites your guests to give each course their full attention.

Gradually, you can "customize" your set and expand its capabilities. Perhaps you saw some really appealing dessert bowls at an antique store or thrift shop. Or maybe some unusual and inepensive salad plates are on sale at a department store. You can use these in conjunction with your set of basic china.

One grandmother gave the wise advice: "Always buy patterns you can afford to replace."

## COORDINATING PATTERNS

The coordination of patterns takes quite a lot of thought. One way to begin is to start with the background color of the primary dishes. For instance, even plain white plates don't all match. There are warm whites and cool, bright whites, and muted whites. The composition of the clay makes a difference, too. Porcelains tend to have a slightly greenish color, because of the clays used in their making. Stoneware is often a little on the gray side of white, and quite opaque. Bone china is the whitest of white.

Pattern and texture are elements that are just as

important as color. An eggshell-thin cup, for example, would look very odd paired with an earthen casserole.

An easy method of coordinating different patterns is to start with the dinner plate and work from there, looking for pleasing combinations of color, texture and pattern. Say that you have a plain white plate with a raised basket-weave design on it. You could easily collect other plates and bowls that also have basket-weave patterns to use for other courses.

Or perhaps you have a white dinner plate with a flower border whose predominant color is pink with green leaves and tiny blue flowers. Green is an obvious color to coordinate, so you could look for green glass or green china salad plates, perhaps in the shape of

leaves. While looking, you might see some pretty pink plates with a flowered center that would be ideal for dessert. Then you might be able to find a bold design featuring all three colors to use for the service plates.

The serving pieces can be coordinated in the same way, using shape, a color or texture as the unifying element.

## THE FIVE-PIECE PLACE SETTING

Most new china is sold in this country in five-piece place settings. The setting consists of a dinner plate, a plate that can be used for salad or dessert, a bread and butter plate, a cup and a saucer. With these basic pieces

❦

MINIMUM CHINA NEEDS PER PERSON

| FOR EVERY DAY | FOR ENTERTAINING |
|---|---|
| Dinner plate | Service plate (optional, for |
| Salad/dessert plate | fancy dinners and buffets) |
| Bread and butter plate (which | Dinner plate |
| can be used for small | Salad/dessert plate |
| desserts) | Bread and butter plate |
| Cereal/soup bowl | Soup bowl |
| Cup and saucer or mug | Coffee cup and saucer |
| Sauce bowl or footed glass | Demitasse cup and saucer |
| bowl for dessert and/or | (optional) |
| appetizer (optional) | |

A guest helping the hostess wash up her heirloom eggshell china held the cups by the handles while drying them—and broke off three handles in succession. Moral: Hold precious cups by the bowl for drying; don't handle the handles.

you can serve a family meal of two courses or a three-course meal without having to wash up bweteen courses. The salad/dessert plate is very useful for breakfast and lunch as well as dinner. You will also need soup and/or cereal bowls, platters and vegetable dishes, either in the same pattern or coordinating ones.

A general rule of quantity for starting out is to figure on at least a dozen place settings of china. You will soon need extra cups and saucers, as these are the first items to get broken. Having extra salad and dessert plates releases you from having to wash up between courses when serving a crowd of people.

## SERVING PIECES

Putting together place settings of china is a simple task compared with the hard work of collecting serving dishes. "Just what items do I need and how do I get them to match?" are the questions almost everyone wants to know.

The answers vary with the kinds of entertaining you find yourself doing, but the following guidelines may help in getting started.

Some people choose to have all their serving pieces in the same pattern as their china, with all bowls, platters and vegetable dishes looking alike. Having everything to match is a good way of making sure that you can always set a balanced and tidy table.

A most interesting or unusual table can be set using unmatched but coordinated serving pieces. A casserole served in a beautiful oven-to-table dish can lift a pleasant-looking table to a dramatic level. A salad served from a shining crystal bowl looks quite different from one tossed in a handsome wooden one, and in either the salad has much more appeal than if it were served in a bowl that demurely matched the china. You might want to serve your Thanksgiving turkey on Great-Aunt Amanda's heirloom platter, and offer the creamed onions in the antique covered vegetable dish you found at the county fair.

Bowls and plates are just a few of the serving pieces that can be used to dramatic effect when setting a table. Trays and baskets can aid in all kinds of ways, and they come in almost infinite variety. Baskets for serving foods are made in just about all sizes, shapes and colors. They can be flat like trays, deep for holding rolls and breads, shallow for a long loaf. These days, baskets are no longer restricted to wicker or rush; materials range from wood to fabric, ceramic, even woven metal.

### MINIMUM SERVING NEEDS

| | |
|---|---|
| 3 vegetable bowls | 1 small platter |
| 1 salad bowl (with or without matching servers, as you prefer) | 3 trays |
| | 1 large platter |
| | 1 baking dish |
| 2 medium-sized baskets for serving breads | 1 cream and sugar set |
| | 1 salt and pepper set |
| 2 covered casserole dishes | |

# CARING FOR CHINA

## WASHING CHINA

- Soak dishes with dried-on food in sudsy water before washing by hand or machine. Never use abrasives such as scouring powder and steel wool on china.
- Cushion the bottom of the sink or dishpan with a rubber mat when washing by hand.
- Wash all antique china, particularly any with gold trim, by hand, using mild detergent and rinsing thoroughly.
- When loading the dishwasher, place the dishes securely in the racks, with enough room between them so that they will not knock or rub against each other during the washing and rinsing cycles.
- Always allow china washed in a dishwasher to cool completely before being stored away.

## STORING CHINA

- When storing fine china, line each plate with a piece of flannel before stacking, or stand the plates sideways in plate racks.
- Hang cups on a cup rack, or stack them no more than two at a time, separated by a piece of flannel.
- When storing china on shelves, allow enough room to keep the pieces from knocking against one another.

Trays for serving drinks, hors d'oeuvres and meal courses come in equally abundant variety. Black lacquer trays show off food dramatically, as do polished silver, brass and copper. Wooden trays have a casual, warm feel that makes them ideal for serving meats, breads, cheeses and vegetables at informal parties and suppers.

# Glassware

The glasses on a table are quite equal to the other elements in importance. Fine stemware makes any table look elegant; hand-blown peasant-style glasses add interest to casual settings. There is no one kind of glassware you *must* have; all glasses share the same attractive properties of shining in the light and showing forth their contents enticingly, once filled. Even the most formal of tables need not be decked with the most expensive crystal, while your champagne flutes can lend an informal setting a dash of the unexpected.

The variety of glassware ranges all the way from cut crystal to the simplest dime-store mass production. Depending on their age, Great-Grandmother's claret glasses would probably fall somewhere in between in your collection. We all use tumblers and juice glasses and have no problem knowing when each is appropriate. But though most of us use wine glasses, there is surprising uncertainty about the shapes and sizes that are appropriate for various occasions.

## THE ALL-PURPOSE WINE GLASS

The most useful shape for entertaining is the basic red wine glass. Larger than the diminutive white wine glass and smaller than the rather unwieldy burgundy glass, it is endlessly adaptable. Almost anything can be served in one, from morning orange juice through to afternoon soft drinks and evening cocktails—and, of course, wine, either white or red—and everything looks good.

Best of all, the basic wine glass need not be expensive. Though, of course, good-quality glass looks lovely on a table, all glassware gleams appealingly. You will want to choose glasses that are not too heavy, so that each glass feels nicely weighted in the hand, and with stems that do not look too coarse. Good examples are to be found in every price range.

## OTHER GLASSES

The only problem with relying on the all-purpose wine glass for most uses is that you need a great many of them if you will be serving guests more than one drink. If you would like some variety, there are, of course, glasses for every possible use.

For people who prefer not to serve cocktails and soft drinks in stemmed glasses, there is a wide selection of other glasses, commonly referred to as barware. The most useful of these are the highball glass, used for tall beverages of all sorts, and the lowball glass, used for short cocktails and non-iced drinks such as morning juices. Highball glasses hold about 12 ounces, lowball glasses, around six ounces.

In the area of stemware, you can choose from a variety of glasses for specific purposes. White wine

Burgundy

Red Wine

White Wine

Highball

glasses, which are a little smaller and sometimes have more rounded bowls than standard red wine glasses, are used for white dinner wines. The glasses that have taller, often colored stems are commonly used for serving German whites, and sweeter dessert wines. The deep round balloon shape of burgundy glasses is designed to let the wine's rich aroma come forth and reach the nose. The same is true of the brandy snifter, so named because the shape of the glass allows you to savor the brandy's fragrance as you warm it in the circle of your hand. Cordials and liqueurs, on the other hand, are served in tiny glasses that invite guests to take gradual sips of the highly fortified contents.

Sherry, which is also a fortified wine, is customarily served before the meal in smaller, stemmed glasses, often slightly fluted in shape.

Champagne flutes, tulips or open coupe glasses are used for champagne and other sparkling wines. Saucer-shaped coupe glasses are the kind that instantly come to mind when we think of champagne, but in fact they

# CARING FOR GLASSWARE

## WASHING GLASSWARE

- It is wisest to wash stemmed glassware by hand, unless you have an unusually deep-shelved dishwasher. When washing glassware by hand, cushion the sink by lining it with a rubber mat.
- Add a few tablespoons of white vinegar to the rinse water to keep crystal brilliant and free of spots.
- Load glasses carefully in the dishwasher to keep them from tapping or rubbing against one another during the washing and rinsing cycles. Glasses should be securely placed on the racks and should not touch one another.
- To clean cloudy vases and decanters, fill with soapy water and add a tablespoon of baking soda. Allow to soak for about 30 minutes. Add a few glass marbles or a tablespoon of raw rice and swirl around to loosen the film. If necessary, allow to soak a little longer and swirl again before rinsing. Be sure the inner surface of a decanter is completely dry before putting back the stopper.
- After washing glassware, allow it to return to room temperature before toweling dry with a lint-free cloth.

## STORING GLASSWARE

- Store crystal right side up with room between the glasses to protect the rims, or hang glasses by the stems from a bar rack.

do not hold the bubbles as satisfactorily as a flute or a tulip-shaped glass. They are adequate for champagne, however, and very useful for such varied purposes as serving seafood appetizers, or soft mousses, puddings and ice cream desserts. Berries and colorful fruit salads show in them to wonderful advantage.

Whatever glasses you use, try to have them match so that everyone at a party can be served in the same pattern. Figure on at least a dozen each of the wine, highball and lowball glasses. For more specialized glasses such as sherry, cordials and brandy snifters, you could start with eight.

## Flatware

If civilization were to be measured by the number of implements used to eat a meal, today's culture would rank well below that of our Victorian forbears. In the days when large staffs of household help were common, the average dinner guest might well be confronted with more than a dozen pieces of silverware in the course of a meal. Such lavishness is rarely seen nowadays, as even our grandest meals tend to be served quite simply.

Though our needs may be fewer, we still are faced with the momentous decision of what kind of flatware to acquire. Varieties of cutlery are available to satisfy every possible taste, from colorful sturdy plastic suitable for outdoor picnics to the finest of hand-wrought silver.

Start by studying your needs now and projecting them into the future. If you are looking for true value, you *have* to consider sterling silver. It is undoubtedly expensive, but it lasts forever, is suitable for almost every occasion, even the most casual, and can even become an heirloom for generations to come.

If immediate economy is a concern, there are many dozens of stainless steel patterns available in all price ranges. Some imitate traditional sterling designs, others are boldly contemporary. Some are nearly as expensive as sterling, others are such bargains that you could even have several to suit various styles of entertaining. Using color-coordinated flatware can be an enjoyable way of accenting the colors you are using to decorate the table.

As with china, you do not have to have everything matching. You could use an antique fish service to serve a first course or even main course, and your grandmother's soup spoons to serve dessert. It is more practical if everyone can use the same pattern of cutlery for each course, but beautiful tables can even be set at which each place setting is different (so long as the elements in the individual settings match each other). Generally speaking, it is better not to mix stainless and silver within a meal, because the styles are quite different, but if that is all the flatware you have and you carry it off with style, your guests will probably think it was planned intentionally.

## WHAT SILVERWARE DO YOU REALLY NEED?

Like china, flatware usually comes in five-piece place settings. These consist of dinner fork, dinner knife, salad fork, soup spoon and teaspoon, which are the essentials needed to serve most meals. Of these, the salad fork—which often serves a first course and dessert function in addition to that of salad—and the teaspoon—which is used at breakfast for cereal, coffee and fruit—are most frequently asked to do extra duty. Of course, though most of us don't, you can also have specific implements for each function. Extras of these two, in particular, will save you having to wash up between courses. In any case, try to plan on at least a dozen full settings.

In addition to the basic settings, you will want serving pieces such as a butter knife for the table (or individual ones), at least three serving spoons (preferably five or six), a serving fork or two, salad servers, a gravy or sauce ladle, a soup ladle and a carving fork and knife.

If you wanted to take care of *every* eventuality, you

*Keep sterling silverware spotless by removing it from the dishwasher just before the drying cycle and wiping each item dry with a soft towel.*

## CARING FOR FLATWARE

### WASHING FLATWARE

- Soak briefly the blades, tines and bowls of knives, forks and spoons that have dried-on food. Do *not* soak the handles of knives that are made in two parts.
- Load stainless steel and sterling silver or silverplate into separate baskets in the dishwasher. Load the baskets with the handles of the knives facing up and the handles of forks and spoons facing down.
- It is wise to wash any precious or antique silver items by hand, especially knives and forks with ivory or bone handles. *Never* allow any two-part items to go through the drying cycle unless you are quite sure they are dishwasher-proof and can handle the heat.

### STORING FLATWARE

- To keep silver from tarnishing, use it. Frequent handling and washing are the best of all tarnish preventatives.
- Polish silver with a soft cloth and mild polish free from any abrasive.
- Store all silver—large pieces as well as flatware—in flannel treated with a tarnish preventative to keep it bright. Enclosing silverware in plastic bags is also effective, because it stops air from reacting with the silver to form tarnish.

could outfit yourself with up to 25 different place setting pieces. Such a set would include:

- eight forks (oyster, snail, fish, luncheon, dinner, salad, dessert and pastry)
- ten spoons (cream soup, bouillon or clear soup, sauce, iced tea, tablespoon, fruit, dessert, ice cream, teaspoon and demitasse spoon)

- seven knives (fish, steak, luncheon, butter, dinner, cheese and fruit)

We won't even discuss the outfit of serving utensils that would accompany what used to be called a "canteen" of cutlery. The word comes from the Italian word *cantina,* meaning cellar—and you would certainly need a cellar to accommodate all the items.

# Linens

The variety of materials available to cover the table is as boundless as your imagination and can include everything from formal linen damask tablecloths to raffia placemats and all manner of things in between, including bed sheets, coverlets and quilts, not to mention more standard cotton and blended cloths.

In some ways, the table covering is the most flexible part of a table setting and the mood of the party can be dictated by the linens you choose. Say the party is a small informal event to herald the coming of spring, it's a drizzly, late-March day and the flowers have a month to go before strutting their stuff. What says "Spring" immediately? Perhaps a light tablecloth made of a length of chintz. You don't have to have special china or crystal or even flowers. The cloth—or it could be placemats—says it all.

Just as you can vary the material to suit your mood, you can have tablecloths in all sizes. Folds that sweep down to the floor can make elegantly luxurious statements; so can pieces of material that don't cover at all, but simply provide a dramatic swath of color or texture.

When a table covering reaches the size of a large place setting, we call it a placemat. Here again, you can create the mood you wish by choosing formal linens,

## CARING FOR LINENS

### GETTING OUT STAINS

- Launder any stained linen as promptly as possible after use.
- To remove grease stains, sprinkle the spot with talcum powder before washing.
- To remove red wine stains, flush the stain with water and then neutralize with a little white wine. You might also try rubbing salt into the stain, then follow up by flushing with water or club soda. After trying either method, soak the cloth overnight in soapy water.
- Treat tomato-based stains by making a paste of laundry detergent and rubbing it well into the stain. Soak the cloth overnight in water before laundering.
- Pouring boiling water from a height of three feet onto blueberry or other berry stains *really does* remove them.

### STORING LINENS

- Store completely dry, ironed tablecloths in a dry place, neatly folded or rolled on a tube.
- Store napkins flat, if you have room to do so. This will leave them without pre-existing fold marks when you come to fold them. Failing that, store them folded in quarters.

casual woven cottons or straw, even lacquered boards. Some people use paper doilies, unfolded napkins or dish towels, a service plate, or nothing at all, choosing, perhaps, to highlight the gleaming surface or pleasing shape of the table itself.

Napkins can make dramatic statements, too. They are essentially there to be useful, of course, but they also provide a wonderfully flexible decorating element. An artfully folded napkin sets the mood of a table just as effectively as an arrangement of flowers or a brilliantly colored tablecloth, and you can change the look in an instant with a new napkin and a fresh fold.

One of the most useful features of napkins is their size. A dozen sets of napkins take up a fraction of the storage space required for several sets of china. You can buy some ultra-chic napkins to set off your classic china and be truly up to date—without having to invest in a trendy china pattern or a brand-new dining room table.

# CHAPTER 3

# SETTING THE TABLE

The sight of a table arranged with abundant silver, china and crystal is certainly impressive. Some people even find it slightly intimidating, which is probably the origin of the notion that there are mysterious rules and customs governing the process of displaying the numerous utensils. In fact, setting a table is done entirely by simple logic, no matter how many items may be in place upon its surface. The purpose of the correctly set table is precisely to guide diners through the meal, making everything they need easy to find and to use.

The logic is based upon the rectangle of space allotted to each person (which is usually about two feet wide). When the diner is seated, everything needed to eat the meal is within reach, or should be. And just as there is no one meal, there is no one way to set a table. The key is to create settings that make immediate sense without explanation, following a familiar pattern, with variations for the different kinds of meals.

*The basic order of use for all meals is to use the
flatware on the outside of the basic rectangle first,
using successive pieces for each course as you move in
toward the plate.*

## THE CASUAL DINNER SETTING

For everyday use, most of us rely on an informal setting
that reflects simple meals of two or three courses. This
is the setting that our mothers taught us when as children we were assigned the task of setting the table
before supper. A setting for a two-course meal—main
course with vegetables (and salad, if one is served) on
the dinner plate, and dessert—usually appears in one of
two ways. If the main course is being served onto plates
by the person seated at the head of the table, the place
setting will consist of a dinner fork, napkin at dead
center, dinner knife, and teaspoon.

When all the food is to be passed, the dinner plate
takes the place of the napkin at dead center, while the
napkin is shifted to the side where the fork is.

Many people have taken up the custom so common in restaurants and now serve salad *before* the main course. This transforms dinner into a three-course meal, and often you will find an extra fork placed to the left of the dinner fork to accommodate the salad. Sometimes salad is served on a separate plate or bowl which is placed to the left and slightly above the forks. It can be served before the main course, or along with it. In the latter case, you will expect to use your dinner fork to eat it and will not need a salad fork.

### SOLVING THE NAPKIN AND FORK DILEMMA

Some people put the napkin *underneath* the fork, but this can be rather awkward because you are supposed to open the napkin and set it upon your knee as soon as you sit down for the meal. To do so, you have to lift the fork—and what should you do then? If you put it down again it could look as if you had made a mistake in picking it up too soon; if you wait with it in your hand, you might seem impatient for your food to be served.

Wise hosts remove the problem by placing the napkin *outside* the setting, to the left of the fork.

In such simple settings there is often one utensil that goes unused—the teaspoon. In households where coffee or tea is routinely drunk with the meal, it will never be idle, and it can also be useful for eating vegetables such as stewed tomatoes or desserts such as custards and puddings or fruit compote. However, when the dessert is cake or pie, or fresh fruit, which are most often eaten with a fork or in the fingers, there will be no use for the lonely teaspoon, and if you elect to do so, you could leave it out of the setting.

Above and to the right of the utensils you will find the water glass and sometimes a wine glass. Glasses always appear above the knife, with the water glass on the left. A small plate of butter (with a knife of its own) often graces the table, as does a salt and pepper set.

A NOTE ABOUT NAPKINS

Many people give dinner napkins very perfunctory treatment at casual meals, just sort of dropping them onto the table. This is quite unfair treatment of an element that can singlehandedly elevate a setting from mundane to inventive. You can loop a napkin through a ring, casually drape it like a scarf, or insert it in the as-yet-to-be-filled water or wine glass (see pages 55 and 56). Nor does the napkin need to rest on the table itself in the traditional fashion. It can be set directly on the dinner plate, draped over the plate's rim, rested at an angle off its edge, or be placed above the setting for a change of pace.

Some people use centerpieces even for family meals, others reserve them for times when there are guests at table.

## THE FESTIVE DINNER SETTING

Any dinner can be festive, whether it is an informal or a high-style affair. In general, though, festive dinners tend more often to be elaborate than casual. Whether given for friends or family or for business reasons, such dinners involve more courses than the usual family meal—up to five or six might be served for a special gathering, though three courses are much more usual—and the courses are almost always distinct from one another. Salad, for instance, will be served on its own on a separate plate or bowl. Informal parties may feature simple china and hand-woven linens, while formal gatherings are natural occasions for displaying the very best linen and porcelain.

For most kinds of parties there is one basic place setting that is logical and easy to use. Like the casual setting, it is based on a rectangle formed by utensils, and it follows the same order of use, with the diner working from the outside in to the center. A fairly standard meal consists of four courses: first course, main course, salad and dessert. Its setting is shown below:

A first course traditionally features soup, fish, shellfish or some other appetizer dish. The soup spoon or shellfish fork to be used for this course are placed on the outside, at the right, where a right-handed person would naturally expect to find them for a course to be eaten with only one hand. If both a knife and fork will be needed, the knife is on the right and the fork on the left.

Working from the left, the remaining utensils are: dinner fork, salad fork (salad is always served *after* the main course when a first course forms part of the menu), dinner plate or service plate, dinner knife, and perhaps a salad knife.

When a meal will have more than three courses the utensils for dessert are placed horizontally, end to end, above the setting, or they may be brought in separately when the dessert is ready to be served. Occasionally, you may see a dessert fork placed to the right of the dinner fork if salad is not being served.

Around the basic setting are a number of other elements. A salad plate might appear to the left of the forks, or it could replace the dinner plate after the entree has been cleared away. A bread and butter plate, often with a butter knife placed on it, may rest on the table above the forks. At a formal dinner, the butter itself is usually found on the individual plate (either as butter pats or neatly sliced in squares); more informally, it will be offered in a butter dish (with a small knife set close by) for the table as a whole.

Directly above the dinner plate might be a place card, an individual salt and pepper set, or perhaps a favor. Placement of the place card varies: it is also sometimes set in the center of the service plate, if one is used, or directly *on* the napkin.

Continuing around the setting to the right, you reach the glasses, which are placed above the knives. The water glass is usually on the left; the wine glasses (see page 28 for which shapes are appropriate for which kinds of wine) are arranged on the right, either in a line or grouped so that they are easy to reach as needed.

### USING SERVICE PLATES

A formal meal is usually set up with a service plate, which is slightly larger than the avera dinner plate, in the center of each place setting. (Service plates are always in a different pattern from the dinner service, but will have been selected to harmonize or contrast with it attractively.) The soup or appetizer is served in a bowl or plate set on top of the service plate. Both will be cleared away when the first course is finished and replaced with the dinner plate (heated if the entree is a hot dish, cold for a main course that will be served chilled).

# A NOTE ABOUT FORMAL SETTINGS

In bygone eras, formal meals were served quite frequently. Today, we rarely see such events save at the most traditional of society functions. The very word "formal" evokes images of rules of propriety and stuffy meals eaten by people wearing full evening dress.

What most of us fail to realize is that a formal table setting is actually simpler than that for a fancy informal dinner. The rules are also more precise.

- A formal table is always set in a simple symmetrical design.
- The table is covered with a white linen cloth and white linen napkins are used, as are fresh white candles.
- The napkin is almost always folded in a simple rectangle.
- A service plate is always used, but the napkin never sits on it, appearing instead to the left of the forks.
- Bread and butter plates are not used, and the salad course is brought in separately after the entree.
- Bowls and platters of food do not appear on the table. All the food is served either plated, or in dishes that are offered individually to each guest by the wait staff.
- The dessert service—dessert plate with fork and spoon—is brought in and set in front of each guest after the table has been cleared of the entree and all its accompaniments.
- Coffee is served as an additional course following dessert, not along with it, and usually in another room.

## SETTING THE BUFFET TABLE

There are two basic ways of handling buffet meals.

When guests will be seated at tables, it is easiest to set the places as for an informal dinner, using the utensils they will need. A buffet usually consists of two courses, so you need only provide silverware for the main entree and dessert. If you will be offering bread with the meal, it is a good idea to place baskets of bread on the tables where people can help themselves once they sit down, to save them from having to juggle slices or rolls on plates already loaded with food.

When diners will be searching out seats for themselves, the entree silverware is usually presented at the end of the buffet table as the last item for guests to pick up as they move along past the various dishes. Dessert silverware is usually presented when the dessert is served.

Use the largest plates you have when serving a buffet. Actual buffet plates, which are slightly larger than dinner plates or service plates, are particularly useful because the larger the plate the easier it is for guests to keep food from spilling.

The way you arrange the food is of primary importance in setting up a buffet table. In many instances it makes sense to set the entree (or entrees) at the head of the table, succeeded by the various vegetables and bread. If an entree is especially rich and should be served in small quantities, you might consider starting with the vegetables and bread so that the plates already look filled when the entree is reached. If you are concerned about portion control, have someone serving at the table. Try to leave ample space between the dishes so that guests can set down their plates and have their hands free for the serving utensils.

If you have invited a large number of people, consider placing the table in the center of the room, and serving from both sides. This will mean, of course, that you will have to set up and serve two versions of every dish so that guests on both sides will have equal opportunities to sample the complete buffet you have prepared. Plan in advance, too, how you will take care of creating additional space for two sets of guests to put their plates down in order to serve themselves.

Place cards can help organize a large party. If you are using them, tell guests in advance, post an easy-to-read seating plan in a visible spot—and carry a copy in your pocket for fast answers.

# THE LUNCHEON SETTING

Luncheon settings, whether for business or pleasure, are usually almost identical to those for a casual supper or a festive dinner. Again, you set out only the utensils that will actually be used in the meal. Such occasions often feature dishes that are lighter than dinner foods. For instance, a salad might well be the main course, which means you would not need separate utensils for salad as well as the entree. You could use salad forks or dinner forks for such a meal. If you happen to possess a set of luncheon silver, which is slightly smaller than dinner silver, this will be the time to use it.

Luncheons, no matter how formal or casual, are often served on placemats rather than tablecloths.

# THE BREAKFAST SETTING

Breakfast is usually the most casual meal of the day. As with all meals, all you really need to provide are the implements required to eat it. At breakfast these can be as simple as one spoon for cereal and another for coffee or tea, a knife and fork if needed, plate and bowl, juice glass, and cup or mug for coffee or tea. Informal though it may be, however, there is no reason not to make breakfast stylish. Even sleepy eaters prefer lifting their own silverware from the setting, and finding a spoon ready to hand by the marmalade jar.

The setting shown here would be suitable for a full-scale breakfast featuring cereal, eggs and ham, fruit, toast and coffee. It consists of napkin, fork, cereal bowl (to be replaced with a plate once finished with), knife, a spoon for fruit and another for cereal. Above the setting are a bread and butter plate for toast (optional) on the left, a juice glass on the right, with a piece of fruit to the right of the juice glass, or in the center of the setting above the plate.

The possibilities for breakfast in bed on a tray are suggested in the other diagram—which does not attempt to include such pleasant additions as the Sunday paper or the book you have been longing to read . . . and plenty of time to enjoy them.

# THE NAPKIN
# FOLDS

## OTHER TRICKS WITH NAPKINS

There are other ways than folds to make a napkin look pretty. Napkin rings, for instance, come in a wide variety of styles: there are straw rings decorated with fruits and flowers, carved ivory rings, wooden rings shaped like animals, mirrored rings, porcelain rings decorated with flowers, metal rings of brass, copper and sterling silver. Any of these can elevate a simply rolled napkin into an artistic statement.

For a simpler, more personal touch, you could tie a piece of ribbon, a length of colored twine, or a strip of green leek or day-lily leaf around your napkins; add a tiny sprig of flowers and you have created yet another special look.

# CHAPTER 4

# FOLDING NAPKINS

The napkin plays the same role in a table setting as the character actor does in a play: it is quite capable of stealing the show, or not, depending on how it is used. A napkin can help create a mood with an obvious statement, if you want it to. The message may be casual or formal, playful or stately, depending on how the fabric has been folded.

You can set a table with a plain square napkin, which shows you intend the meal to be strictly businesslike. Or you can decorate the settings with fanciful creations designed to suit a meal over which you have taken special pains. By taking equal care with the napkins, you show your guests that you intend for them to dine—not just eat—and to share the company and conversation of fellow friends.

All this can be achieved with just a few extra minutes of preparation time. But what do you use and how do you start?

Begin with the napkins themselves.

**51**

When using
material printed
on one side,
remember that
some folds show
both sides of the
napkin; this can
sometimes add
the illusion of two
different fabrics,
other times it can
look ineffective.
Select a fold that
shows the
material to its
best advantage.

In general, the larger the napkin, the easier it is to fold. Some folds can be quite elaborate, requiring a fair amount of fabric. More complicated folds usually need full dinner-sized napkins that are at least 17 inches square. Simpler folds are often most suitable for small-sized napkins, the kind you might use for luncheon or a light meal. All napkins must be square, or easily folded into a large square.

The texture of the fabric is also extremely important. Brand-new napkins are the easiest to fold, as they are usually stiff enough to hold a crease, but not so stiff as to rebound and spring flat again. Heavily starched linen, unstarched linen and synthetic materials are sometimes hard to fold, though for different reasons. Highly starched and synthetic fabric napkins tend to have too much spring to hold the firm creases required to make the folds. Unstarched linen and light cotton napkins often do not have enough body to take crisp creases and folds. You can find a middle ground by using napkins made of lightly starched linen or cotton, or medium-weight cotton, lightly starched and/or freshly ironed, or soft synthetic fabrics.

What fabrics are suitable for napkins and napkin folding? There is a wide range to choose from. Classic linen napkins always look and feel good, as do ones made from good-quality cotton. Bandannas, jacquard and striped dish towels, squares of striped or checked seersucker, handwoven fabrics, printed chintzes and calicos, and a host of other textured fabrics and prints all make attractive napkins.

Experiment with the folds that follow to see which ones best suit your styles of entertaining and the fabrics you have available. You can practice with paper napkins to see how the folds actually work out, but paper is ineffective for anything other than the simplest folds because it has no texture. The ideal practice material to use for the more formal folds is an old, well starched dinner napkin, the kind our grandmothers used for special occasions, made of heavy damask linen, which can accept being manipulated into quite complicated shapes and still look gracious and elegant.

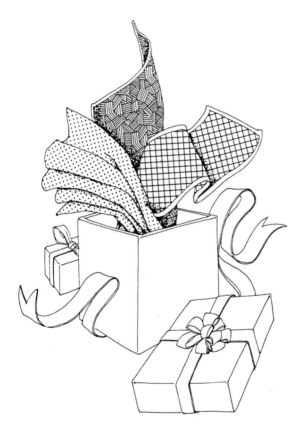

# CHAPTER 5

# EVERYDAY FOLDS

E very one of these folds is extremely straightforward, yet each adds a different touch to the table. It is as easy to fold a stylish napkin as to set out a plain oblong or square at family mealtimes, and you may be surprised to find how many people are interested in the art.

## The Swirl

This casual but stylish fold is suitable for almost any kind of informal dinner, supper, picnic or lunch. It takes just moments to roll, yet gives the instant impression that you have taken trouble to make your table look attractive. It can be done with a simple printed napkin, or a more formal fabric. The more casual the fabric, the more informal the look.

1. Lay the napkin out flat.

2. Starting with one of the corners, roll the napkin up.

3. Bend the napkin in the middle and place it in a glass.

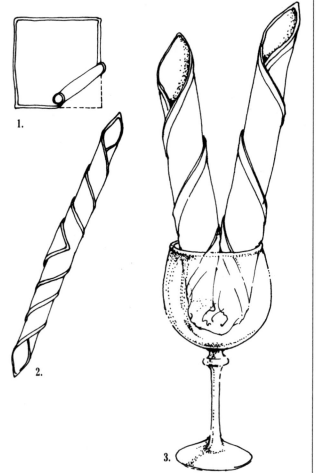

1.

2.

3.

A stemmed glass looks best with a light fabric roll; if you are using heavier material, you might prefer a sturdier glass.

# The Fan in a Glass

This is an invaluable fold to have in your repertoire. It is extremely simple, which makes it ideal for breakfast either in bed or at the table, and can be inserted in the juice glass placed in the center of the setting. But its simplicity also makes it useful for more formal occasions, when you want to take time to concentrate on other elements in the setting or the meal, yet still cut a dash with a handsome-looking napkin.

1. Fold the napkin in half.
2. Make a series of one-inch-wide accordion pleats all the way up the napkin.
3. Hold the pleats together at the folded side and slip this end into a glass. Let the pleats open up and dispose them attractively above the glass.

You can vary the look of this fan by using different-sized glasses and napkins. A bigger napkin, for example, will give a fuller, more ruched effect in a taller glass.

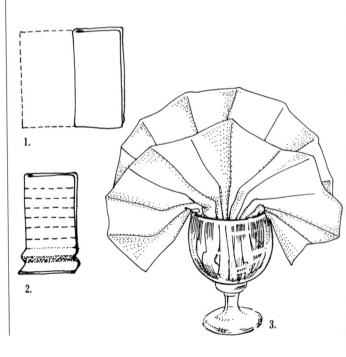

1.

2.

3.

# The Scarf

This is a useful fold for a festive informal table setting, at a holiday breakfast time, for example. It can be placed at the center of the setting or at the left-hand side.

1. Fold the napkin into quarters.
2. Fold it in half diagonally.
3. Pleat each half, as shown.
4. Slip the napkin through a napkin ring or tie it with a ribbon.

Is this the time to polish up your heirloom silver rings and use them? Or to tie colored ribbons around each napkin, labeled with a name and a message? Only you can know.

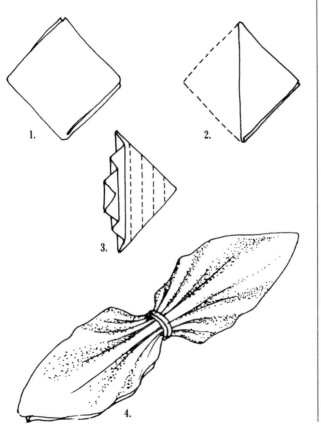

# The Book

The Book is a simple fold that produces a look of leaved pages. It is useful for lunch or brunch—even supper—settings, and since its look is casual, it can be made from almost any kind of napkin, from a crisp linen to a soft cotton.

1. Fold the napkin into thirds.

2. Fold first the left and then the right sides over one quarter.

3. Fold both sides over again so that they meet in the center.

4. Lift the napkin and fold the right side back under the left.

5. Slide the napkin sideways to display three equal folds.

This can look quite formal made with a damask or embroidered linen napkin set in front of the guest, with a place card or menu inserted in one of the folds.

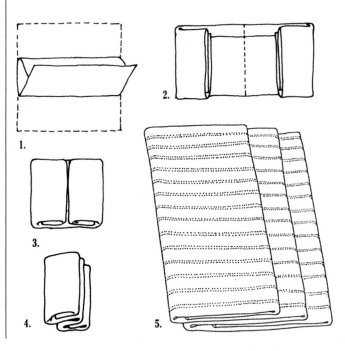

# The Ascot Tie

This is a delightful fold—festive, yet casual, and suitable for many occasions. One of its best features is that it can be made from crisp fabrics, but also looks terrific when folded from paper napkins.

1. Fold the napkin in half diagonally.
2. Fold the bottom edge up by one quarter; fold it up again by one quarter.
3. Fold the sides over, as shown.
4. Turn the napkin over and lay it flat.

Because this fold lies flat, the napkin can be folded ahead of time and put into the picnic hamper, all ready to go.

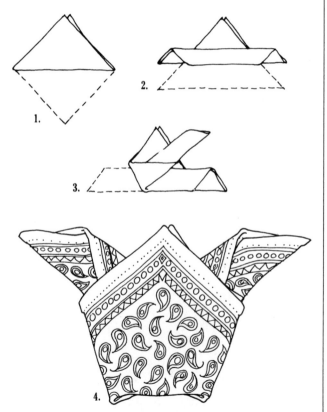

# The Classic Fold

For a truly formal dinner, at which only white damask table linens, the finest silver and the simplest of decorations are used, only one napkin fold is appropriate. It is the easiest of all and the most elegant because of its simplicity.

1. Fold the napkin in half horizontally.
2. Fold it in half again, vertically.
3. Fold the napkin in half again, bringing the right-hand side over the left.

For a fold so starkly simple, every napkin must be in tiptop shape, exquisitely ironed and folded. Embroidery or initials should end up in the lower left-hand corner of each finally folded napkin. Subtlety shows at times like this.

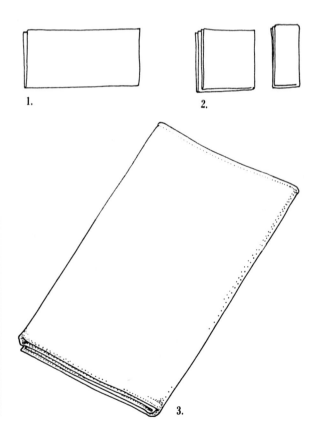

1.

2.

3.

# A la Maison

Afternoon tea, in its most proper form, is a rather formal affair. That, after all, is what makes it an event rather than a simple mug of hot tea and a cookie in the late afternoon. This fold is simple yet elegant, just like the party, and lends itself with equal grace to napkins embroidered or trimmed with lace and to more informal, brightly flowered chintzes.

    1. Fold the napkin into quarters with the loose ends upward.

    2. Turn up the bottom corner.

    3. Fold the sides over to form thirds.

    4. Turn the napkin over and lay it flat.

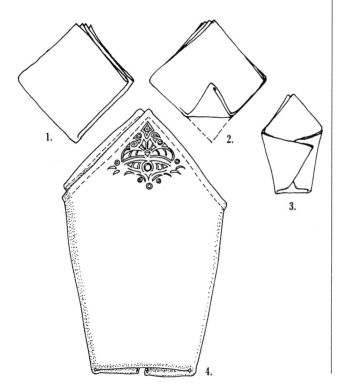

# The Havana

This is another extremely useful and decorative fold that is formed in a trice and looks better than nice.

　　1. Fold the napkin into quarters with the free corners at the bottom.

　　2. Fold the top flap up one half.

　　3. Fold each of the remaining flaps up to fall one inch lower than the previous flap, as shown.

　　4. Fold back the sides and lay the napkin flat.

The only problem with this fold is stopping yourself from using it on every occasion. Like the Ascot Tie (page 59), it lends itself to being made in paper, ahead of time, and packed for a picnic.

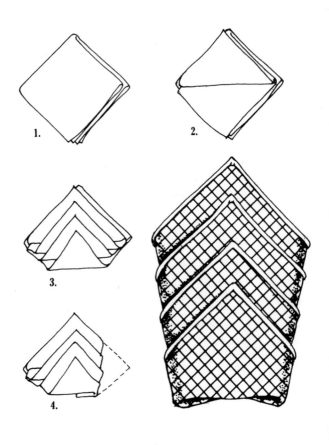

1.

2.

3.

4.

# CHAPTER 6

# FANCY FOLDS

N othing gives a broader scope for fancy napkin folds than a festive dinner. You could be entertaining the boss, celebrating a special event, or just creating a romantic evening. For those times when you go all out in entertaining, some of these impressive, formal-looking folds can give the finishing touch to the decorated table.

# The Bishop's Hat

This is probably the most impressive fold of them all. Though you have probably seen it carried out in the classic fashion with big, white, stiffly starched damask napkins, it can look equally superb folded from delicate stiff muslin napkins in, say, a striking fuchsia pink or cornflower blue.

    1. Fold the napkin in half diagonally to form a triangle.

    2. Fold the left and right corners up to meet at the top point. This will form a diamond shape.

    3. Fold the bottom corner up to about one inch below the top.

    4. Fold the corner back to the bottom edge.

    5. Turn the napkin over, bring each of the sides back and tuck one of them into the other.

    6. Stand the napkin upright and tuck each of the flaps down into the cuff.

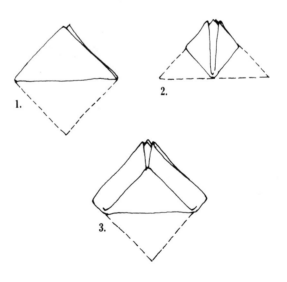

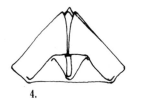

4.

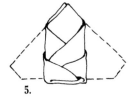

5.

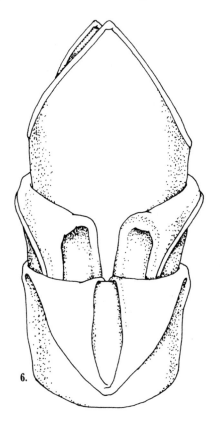

6.

# The Rose

This seems like a very complicated design to achieve, but it is quite straightforward provided you take each of the steps in sequence. You will need a glass to hold the center of each napkin down while you form the rose shape around it.

The Rose seems a natural fold for a flowered chintz, say, or a pastel print. But it can take on quite a different, ultra-modern look made from a fabric in a striking geometric design.

1. Fold each of the napkin's four corners to the center.

2. Repeat the step with the new corners.

3. Repeat Step 1 again with the corners formed in Step 2.

4. Holding the folds down, turn the napkin over very carefully. Fold all four corners to the center again.

5. Place a glass in the center of the napkin to hold down the folds. Pull out each of the corners in turn from the underside with a light tug to make each one stand up.

6. Remove the glass and, holding the center of the napkin together with your hand, turn it over again.

7. Pull up each of the flaps in the center to form the petals of the Rose.

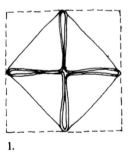

1.

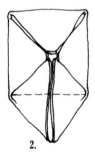

2.

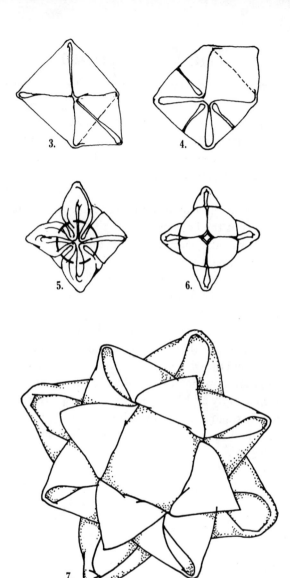

3.

4.

5.

6.

7.

# The Cockscomb

Lunches on special occasions, whether they are being given for business or pleasure, deserve to be dressed up with an intriguing fold such as The Cockscomb. For some people it evokes the image of an exotic flower, beckoning the guest to sit.

1. Fold the napkin into quarters with the free corners at the bottom.

2. Bring the bottom half of the napkin up to the top, forming a triangle.

3. Fold first the left and then the right side to the center. (Each will hang down below the basic triangle.)

4. Fold the extended pieces back underneath the napkin, so that it forms a triangle again.

5. Fold the triangle in half vertically, then stand it upright horizontally, as shown. (The napkin will open slightly at the center; pinch a crisp crease to help it stand without spreading.)

6. Pull up each of the free flaps in turn.

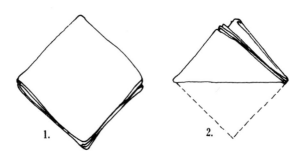

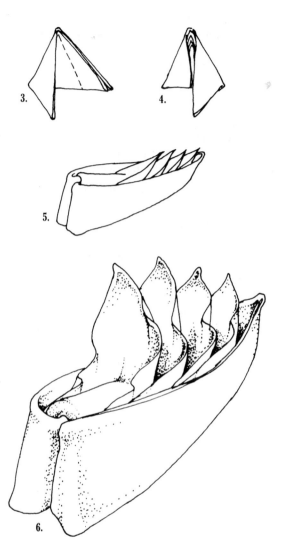

3.

4.

5.

6.

This jaunty fold works best when made with a fairly large napkin that accepts a firm crease. It also looks striking made with a good-quality paper napkin in a strong color.

# The Buffet Server

One of the elements to consider when setting up a buffet is how to make it easy for the guests to manage the equipment. The most sensible solution is to wrap the silverware in the napkin. The simplest method is to roll up the silver inside the napkin, but guests may find the unrolling awkward to handle. The Buffet Server is a much more stylish solution, which highlights the silverware as well as the napkin, and can be made equally well with cloth or paper napkins.

If you like, you can add a Step 2A, and fold the remaining flap down to meet the crease you have just made. This makes the napkin/cutlery packet more compact and can be very effective with a napkin that has striking borders.

1. Fold the napkin in half.

2. Fold the top flap back down to the bottom crease.

3. Turn the napkin over and fold first the left and then the right-hand side in half vertically to meet in the middle. Overlap one with the other and insert the utensils in the pocket.

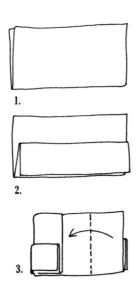

1.

2.

3.

# The Surprise Package

Festively shaped paper napkins can play a crucial role in the decoration of a children's birthday party table. Either of the two folds that follow can be coordinated either by color or motif with the general theme you have selected for the party, and will generate a lot of excitement on their own.

1. Fold the napkin into quarters with the free corners at the top.

2. Fold the bottom and side corners to the center.

3. Turn the napkin over and fold the first flap down halfway.

4. Insert a surprise.

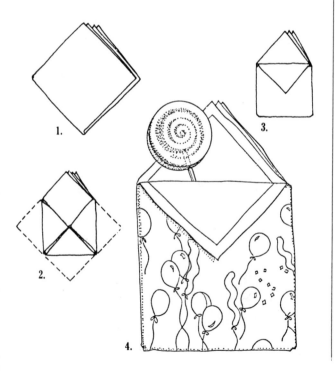

The surprise can stick up, as shown, or you could enclose a hidden treasure, with a big shiny sticker holding the other flaps down over the "envelope."

# The Paper Pinwheel

The Pinwheel shown here looks spectacular and sports a tiny party favor at its center—a piece of candy, a special button, or a small toy.

1. Fold the left and right corners to the center.

2. Turn the napkin over and fold the top and bottom corners to the center.

3. Turn the napkin so that one of the corners faces you, then fold the top and bottom corners to the center.

4. Turn the napkin over and fold the side corners to the center.

5. Pull out each of the corners marked with a dot in the first diagram, as shown in the second one.

6. Turn the napkin over again and pull out each of the corners marked with a dot. The favor you put in the center will help hold the folds down.

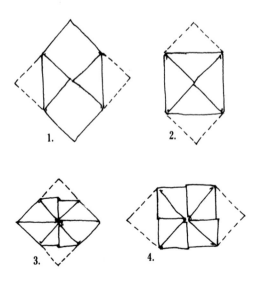

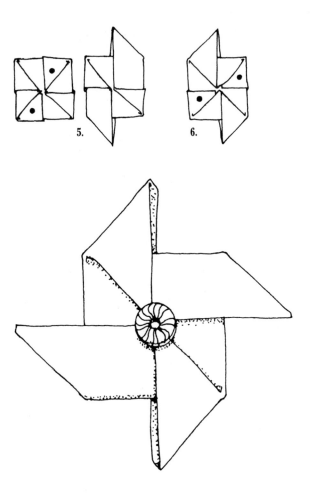

5.

6.

# The Standing Fan

A table dressed for Thanksgiving always looks special—the glorious, perfectly browned turkey is certainly one of its top attractions—and it provides an opportunity for an appropriately festive fold. The Standing Fan even looks a little like the majestic plumage of the noble bird.

1. Fold the napkin in half.

2. Make a series of one-inch accordion pleats, starting at the left and leaving about four inches at the right.

3. Fold the napkin in half with the pleats facing out and with the bend on the bottom.

4. Holding the pleats together at the top, fold the back down on each side to form a triangle, and tuck each in turn behind the center pleats you are holding. This will form the stand.

5. Stand the napkin up, allowing the pleats to form a fan.

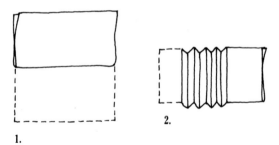

1.

2.

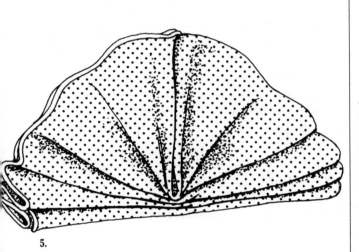

3.

4.

5.

This is best made
with stiffly
starched napkins;
if they are at all
limp you may
need to use a clip
to hold the fan's
center together.

# The Fleur-de-Lys

The original name for this fold comes from the fleur-de-lis or medieval lily, which was the emblem of the kings of France. It turns the simplicity of the Fan in a Glass (page 56) into a sophisticated table decoration simply by basing itself on a triangle rather than a square—and it does end up looking like a lovely flower.

1. Fold the napkin in half diagonally.

2. Fold the bottom edge up to meet the top point, as shown.

3. Fold the edge back on itself, leaving about an inch at the bottom.

4. Fold in one-inch-wide accordion pleats from left to right.

5. Pinch the pleats together at the bottom and slip into a glass. Allow the top to fan out and pull out the side "leaves."

This fold can easily be adapted to stand upright in a napkin ring if you fold the bottom edge up about three inches in Step 2 and omit Step 3.

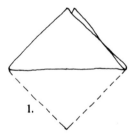

1.

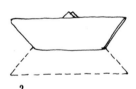

2.

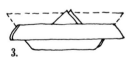

3.

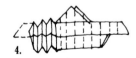

4.

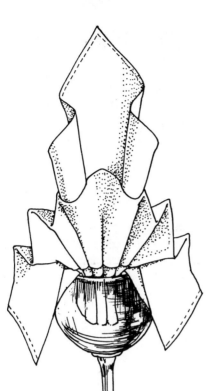

5.

# The Bottle Scarf

This is an extremely useful fold for any occasion when you are serving from bottles, and the type of napkin you use can set exactly the style you want: from gingham or a bandanna all the way up to white damask.

1. Fold the napkin in half diagonally.
2. Fold the bottom edge up by one quarter twice.
3. Tie the napkin around the bottle and fold the points down toward the base.

To catch condensation from a chilled bottle, turn back one of the points over the band formed after Step 2, set the bottle on the other flap and then wrap the band around the bottle. Take care to catch the rear flap as you tie the napkin in a secure knot.

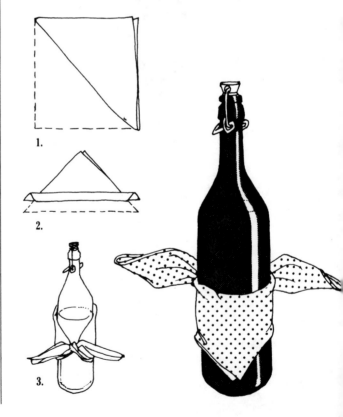

1.

2.

3.

# INDEX